Cancún & The Riviera Maya Easy Guide

Unveiling The Enchanting Secrets Of The Mexican Caribbean - A Simple Travel Guide

Rachel Hendrick

Copyrighted material

Copyright © 2023 Rachel Hendrick.
All rights reserved.

Protected by copyright law and international treaties, this book includes all materials, texts, pictures, drawings, maps, logos, and design elements.

No part of this publication may be reproduced, distributed, or transmitted in any form or by any means, including photocopying, recording, or other electronic or mechanical methods, without the prior written permission of the publisher, except in the case of brief quotations embodied in critical reviews and certain other noncommercial uses permitted by copyright law.

Copyrighted material

Table of contents

Introduction 4
Chapter 1: Getting to Know the Mexican Caribbean... 9
    Welcome to Cancún & The Riviera Maya 13
    The Rich History and Culture of the Region 16
    Climate and Best Travel Periods 18
    Important Travel Advice for a Painless Experience 21
Chapter 2: Showcasing the Best of Cancún 26
    Unveiling the Marvels of Cancún's Beaches 27
    Landmarks and Attractions You Must Visit 31
Chapter 3: The Wonders of the Riviera Maya 35
    Discovering Ancient Mayan Ruins and Archaeological Sites 36
    Embracing Nature: Eco Parks, Cenotes, and Wildlife Reserves 39
    Enjoying Peace in Calm Beaches and Coastal Towns 43
Chapter 4: Outdoor Activities and Adventure 47
    Aquatic Adventures and Exciting Water Sports 48
    Exploring the Lush Jungles and Zip-Lining through Nature 51
    Scuba and Snorkeling in the Caribbean Sea: A Diver's Paradise 55
Chapter 5: Indulging in Mexican Caribbean Flavors... 59
    Mexican Cuisine: A Gastronomic Tour 60
    Best Restaurants, Food Markets, and Street Eats. 63

Copyrighted material

    Indulging in Regional Delicacies and Refreshing Beverages..66

Chapter 6: Useful Preparation for a Memorable Trip.. 70

    Choosing the Right Accommodations: Resorts, Hotels, and Rentals... 71

    Navigating Transportation and Getting Around the Area.. 75

    Tips for Safety and Health for a Worry-Free Vacation 79

Chapter 7: Beyond Cancun & The Riviera Maya..... 84

    Day Trips to Nearby Islands and Charming Coastal Towns... 85

    Exploring the Yucatán Peninsula's Hidden Gems.. 88

    Extending Your Adventure to Other Alluring Mexican Destinations... 93

Chapter 8: Helpful Resources and Information....... 97

    Language Guide and Communication Tips............ 98

    Travelers' Money and Currency Issues................ 102

    List of Things to Pack and Travel Essentials........ 105

Maps of Mexican Caribbean.................................... 110

Conclusion and final Thought for an Unforgettable Experience..111

Copyrighted material

Introduction

Welcome to "Cancún & The Riviera Maya Easy Guide" - your ultimate companion to uncovering the enchanting secrets of the Mexican Caribbean. This comprehensive travel guide is meticulously crafted to provide you with an immersive experience, delving into the captivating destinations of Cancún and the scenic wonders of the Riviera Maya.

Imagine stepping into a realm where turquoise waters kiss powdery white shores, ancient ruins

Copyrighted material

narrate tales of civilizations past, and vibrant cultures infuse every moment with vibrant energy. From the moment you set foot in this tropical paradise, you'll be captivated by the sheer beauty and diversity that await you.

Our journey begins with an enticing introduction to the Mexican Caribbean, where we invite you to embrace the allure of Cancún and the Riviera Maya.

From the bustling city of Cancún, renowned for its stunning beaches and lively nightlife, to the serene coastal towns along the Riviera Maya, steeped in rich history and culture, each destination beckons with its unique charm.

Throughout this guide, we will unlock a treasure trove of experiences, guiding you through the must-visit landmarks and attractions that have earned Cancún its reputation as a world-class destination. You'll uncover the mysteries of ancient Mayan ruins and archaeological sites, connecting with the vibrant history that shaped this region.

For nature enthusiasts, we have curated a chapter devoted to the wonders of the Riviera Maya. Explore the lush eco-parks, mystical cenotes, and wildlife reserves that will immerse you in the breathtaking natural beauty of this land. Tranquil beaches invite you to unwind and recharge, leaving behind the worries of the world.

For those seeking a dose of adrenaline, "Adventure and Outdoor Activities" is your gateway to thrilling water sports and zip-lining through the dense jungles, providing an exhilarating contrast to the tranquil coastline.

And what journey to the Mexican Caribbean would be complete without savoring the exquisite flavors of the region? In the "Savoring the Flavors of the Mexican Caribbean" chapter, embark on a gastronomic journey through the richness of Mexican cuisine. We'll guide you to the best restaurants, hidden food markets, and authentic street eats, ensuring that every meal becomes a delightful experience.

Practicality is at the core of our guide, with a dedicated chapter to help you plan a seamless trip. From choosing the right accommodations, whether luxurious resorts or cozy hotels, to navigating transportation to make the most of your time, we provide you with the tools to craft an unforgettable vacation.

Venturing "Beyond Cancún & The Riviera Maya," we'll introduce you to delightful day trips to nearby islands and charming coastal towns, as well as hidden gems scattered across the Yucatán Peninsula. Extend your adventure to other alluring Mexican destinations, allowing you to explore more of the country's breathtaking landscapes and diverse cultures.

Copyrighted material

To ensure you're well-prepared, our guide offers valuable resources, including a language guide for effective communication, currency, and money matters, and a packing checklist to equip you with all the essentials for your journey.

Embark on this immersive journey with us, as we take you on a voyage through the enchanting secrets of the Mexican Caribbean. Whether you're a seasoned traveler or setting out on your first adventure, "Cancún & The Riviera Maya Easy Guide" promises to be your trusted companion, igniting your wanderlust and leaving you with cherished memories that will last a lifetime. Let the journey begin!

Copyrighted material

Chapter 1: Getting to Know the Mexican Caribbean

The Mexican Caribbean beckons with its irresistible allure, offering a mesmerizing tapestry of pristine beaches, rich history, and vibrant culture. Embarking on this journey begins with accessing the gateway to this tropical paradise. Let's delve into the cities that compose the magical Mexican Caribbean.

Cancún, a name synonymous with paradise, welcomes you with its azure waters and golden shores. This bustling city is renowned for its luxury resorts, exciting nightlife, and a wide array of activities to indulge in. Whether you're seeking a tranquil beach retreat or an adventure-packed escapade, Cancún sets the stage for an unforgettable experience.

As we venture further south, the Riviera Maya unfurls its wonders before our eyes. Playa del Carmen, a vibrant coastal town, entices visitors with its bohemian atmosphere, boutique shops, and trendy beach clubs. Picture yourself strolling along its bustling Quinta Avenida, where the vibrant energy of the Caribbean merges with the laid-back charm of a beachside town.

Just a stone's throw away lies Tulum, a treasure trove of ancient ruins and archaeological sites. Immerse yourself in the echoes of the past as you explore the enigmatic Mayan ruins perched atop cliffs overlooking the

Caribbean Sea. Tulum's bohemian spirit and eco-consciousness create a unique blend of history and modernity.

Venturing further south, we encounter the picturesque town of Akumal, a paradise for snorkeling enthusiasts. Dive into crystal-clear waters teeming with marine life, including sea turtles that grace these coastal shores. Akumal's relaxed ambiance invites you to slow down and savor every moment by the sea.

Moving on, the laid-back charm of Puerto Morelos awaits. Discover a fishing village where time seems to stand still, offering a peaceful respite from the bustling cities. Here, you can embrace the simplicity of life, enjoying the pristine beaches and mingling with friendly locals.

Further south lies the captivating city of Chetumal, the capital of Quintana Roo. Embrace the blend of modernity and tradition as you explore the city's museums, bustling markets, and vibrant cultural scene. Chetumal's proximity to the Belize border adds an international flavor to its atmosphere.

As we reach the southernmost point, Bacalar enchants with its stunning lagoon, known as the "Lagoon of Seven Colors." The kaleidoscope of turquoise hues makes it a surreal and mesmerizing destination, ideal for relaxation and water-based activities.

With its distinctive cities and unique charms, the Mexican Caribbean promises an adventure like no other. Whether you seek relaxation, cultural exploration, or thrilling experiences, each city contributes its chapter to this captivating story. So pack your bags and embark on a journey to the Mexican Caribbean, where unforgettable memories await at every turn.

Welcome to Cancún & The Riviera Maya

Welcome to the mesmerizing world of Cancún and the captivating wonders of the Riviera Maya. This is a realm where sun-kissed beaches meet ancient ruins, where vibrant nightlife harmonizes with tranquil coastal towns, and where nature's beauty and human history blend seamlessly.

As you step foot into Cancún, the energy of this bustling city will engulf you. Feel the soft sand beneath your toes as you stroll along the shimmering coastline, and let the warm tropical breeze brush against your skin. With its luxurious resorts, vibrant entertainment, and an array of water sports, Cancún offers an irresistible invitation to indulge in paradise.

The Riviera Maya, stretching southward from Cancún, unravels like a vibrant tapestry of natural wonders and cultural treasures. Playa del Carmen, a bohemian beach town, charms visitors with its artistic flair and laid-back ambiance. Quinta Avenida, the bustling main street, entices a medley of shops, restaurants, and colorful street performances.

Explore the captivating mysteries of Tulum, where ancient Mayan ruins stand proudly atop coastal cliffs, gazing out over the turquoise Caribbean waters. The blend of history and natural beauty in Tulum creates an enchanting ambiance that lingers in the hearts of travelers.

Journeying onward, you'll find Akumal, a hidden gem for snorkeling enthusiasts. Glide through pristine waters alongside graceful sea turtles, and immerse yourself in the tranquil rhythm of this coastal paradise.

Puerto Morelos, a fishing village with a serene charm, invites you to unwind and savor life's simple pleasures. Discover its laid-back atmosphere, enjoy fresh seafood by the sea, and feel the stress of everyday life dissipate.

Chetumal, the capital of Quintana Roo, presents a blend of modernity and traditional heritage. The city's museums, markets, and cultural events provide a glimpse into the dynamic spirit of the region.

Reach the breathtaking Bacalar, home to the "Lagoon of Seven Colors." Be mesmerized by the kaleidoscope of hues reflected in the lagoon's crystal-clear waters, an awe-inspiring sight that seems almost surreal.

So, immerse yourself in the rich history, vibrant culture, and breathtaking landscapes that await you. Allow the Mexican Caribbean to awaken your senses and ignite your spirit of exploration. The enchanting allure of Cancún and the Riviera Maya is yours to discover.

The Rich History and Culture of the Region

Travelers from all over the world are enthralled by the rich history and culture of the Mexican Caribbean. The mighty Mayan civilization once ruled this area, leaving behind a legacy of stunning archaeological sites and historic ruins that depict a bygone age.

You will be in amazement when you tour the Riviera Maya and Cancún to see the remains of this historic culture. One of the New Seven Wonders of the World, the renowned Chichen Itza is a UNESCO World Heritage site. Its magnificent pyramid, known as El Castillo or the Temple of Kukulcan, demonstrates the great astronomical knowledge and intricate building abilities of the Maya.

Make the trip to Tulum, a coastal wonder whose ruins are located on cliff tops with views

Copyrighted material

of the Caribbean Sea. You can envision the bustling port metropolis that formerly inhabited this area thanks to the structures' excellent preservation, which takes you back in time.

Beyond the impressive archaeological monuments, the culture of the Mexican Caribbean is thriving today. You are greeted with open arms by the friendly locals, and you feel at home because of their real friendliness. You'll be surrounded by the vibrant Mexican culture, from the vibrant customs and celebrations to the vivacious music and dance.

A significant aspect of the local culture is the delicious blend of indigenous ingredients and Spanish influences that is Mexican food. Each mouthful of foods like tacos, enchiladas, and tamales offers a taste of heritage and history as you savor their exquisite flavors.

The culture of the Mexican Caribbean is a seamless fusion of historic origins and modern influences, where the past and present coexist. Every move you make unveils a new layer of the region's compelling past, making history come alive there.

You will go on a journey of discovery as you delve into the rich history and culture of the Mexican Caribbean and come to understand the spirit of a place that has proudly retained its legacy. Take in the beauty of this cultural tapestry and allow it to absorb you; in doing so, you will have a deeper understanding of and appreciation for the splendor of the Mexican Caribbean.

Climate and Best Travel Periods

An enjoyable and memorable journey requires knowledge of the environment and selecting the optimum time to visit the Mexican Caribbean. Your experience is greatly influenced by the seasonal and meteorological variations in the area. Let's simplify it so you can make informed visit planning decisions.

The Mexican Caribbean's Climate:

A tropical climate, with consistently warm temperatures and high humidity levels, prevails throughout the Mexican Caribbean. There are two distinct seasons in the area:

Dry Season (November to April): Due to the normally sunny and dry weather, this is the season when tourists are most active. The ideal environment for beach activities, water sports, and the exploration of ancient sites is provided by moderate to warm temperatures.

Rainy Season: From May through October, the area sees higher humidity levels and sporadic precipitation, frequently in the form of brief, powerful showers. While the rain provides welcome relief from the heat, it is imperative to be ready for sporadic inclement weather.

Ideal Seasons to Visit:

Your interests and priorities will play a big part in determining the best time to travel to the Mexican Caribbean. Here are two simple models to aid in your decision-making:

Plan Your vacation around the Dry Season, from November to April, for the Best Weather: If you enjoy sunny days with little possibility of rain, plan your vacation around this time. The best weather for outdoor activities, relaxing on the beach, and taking in the region's attractions is during this time.

Consider going During the **Rainy Season**, May to October, for Less Crowds and More Economical Options: If you want a more laid-back and economical experience, consider going during the rainy season, May to October. Even though it can rain, this time of year usually has fewer visitors, which means shorter lineups at popular attractions and cheaper prices on lodging and activities.

Tropical Storm Season:
The official hurricane season, which extends from June to November, should be understood. Although the Mexican Caribbean is well-equipped to deal with these circumstances, it is advisable to stay up to current on weather reports and any travel warnings at this time.

You may customize your vacation to meet your interests and expectations by being aware of the weather patterns and ideal times to visit.

Important Travel Advice for a Painless Experience

- ❖ Keep Your Travel Documents Safe:
- ❖ Verify that your passport is still valid for at least six months after the date you want to travel. Important documents should be

copied and stored separately from the originals. For easy access, keep digital copies on your phone or in the cloud.

- ❖ Make Transportation Plans in Advance: Look into your choices for getting from the airport to your lodging. If you want to travel outside of the major cities, think about making a reservation for a reputable airport transfer service or renting a car.
- ❖ Maintain Hydration and Sun Protection: Tropical weather in the Mexican Caribbean can be severe. Drink a lot of water throughout the day to stay hydrated. To protect yourself from the sun's rays, remember to frequently apply sunscreen and don a hat and sunglasses.
- ❖ Accept the Local Currency and Language: A few simple Spanish words

might help you communicate with locals and get by in ordinary life. Know the Mexican Peso, the local currency, and carry small denominations for ease.

- ❖ Use Caution When Using Ice and Tap Water: Stick to drinking and brushing your teeth with bottled or filtered water to avoid any potential health risks. Ice in beverages should be used with caution because it isn't always created with pure water.
- ❖ Use responsible tourism tactics: Be mindful of the environment and cultural traditions. When visiting archaeological sites, abide by the rules and never disturb the wildlife or remove any artifacts. Select eco-friendly pursuits and assist neighborhood enterprises.
- ❖ Maintain Your Safety Knowledge: While it's generally safe to travel in the Mexican

Caribbean, it's important to be aware of any security issues in the area. As you would in any other place, use reliable sources for travel advice and be cautious overall.

- ❖ Keep Your Day Bag With Essentials: Keep the necessities in a day bag, including sunscreen, water, a cap, snacks, and a map or guidebook. On excursions and during explorations, this will be useful.
- ❖ Make wise use of the regional cuisine: Enjoy the delectable Mexican food, but be cautious when eating it on the street. To assure cleanliness and freshness, choose food vendors with a large turnover of customers.
- ❖ Be Receptive to Cultural Diversity: Accept the cultural traditions and customs of the area. Be respectful of

regional customs while remaining receptive to new foods, music, and festivities.

- ❖ Tipping manners: The Mexican Caribbean region has a tipping culture. In restaurants, a gratuity of between 10% and 15% of the tab is customary. Tip tour operators and drivers according to the quality of their services.
- ❖ Keep Informed and Connected: Have a dependable way to stay in touch while traveling, such as a local SIM card or an international data package. Utilize travel applications and internet tools to stay up to date on regional events and activities.

You'll have a smooth and joyful experience discovering the beauties of the Mexican Caribbean if you adhere to this crucial travel advice.

Copyrighted material

Chapter 2: Showcasing the Best of Cancún

A tropical oasis located along Mexico's Caribbean coast, Cancún invites a variety of alluring attractions. The following places and activities are absolute must-sees that will make your trip unforgettable:

Copyrighted material

Unveiling the Marvels of Cancún's Beaches

The beaches of Cancún are a magical wonder that attracts tourists from all over the world. A paradise of soft, powdery sands and turquoise, crystal-clear waters may be found along the unspoiled coastline. Let's investigate what makes Cancún's beaches so alluring as we delve into their wonders:

- ❖ Delfines Playa: Playa Delfines is a well-liked destination for both locals and tourists because of its recognizable "Cancún " sign. It is a great spot for beachgoers to unwind, snap pictures, and take in the splendor of nature because of the expansive views of the Caribbean Sea and the lively ambiance.
- ❖ Playa Turtles: Playa Tortugas is the place to go for a more peaceful getaway. This

calm beach offers a tranquil atmosphere, making it perfect for relaxing with a good book under the shade of palm trees or taking strolls down the shore.

- ❖ Beach Forum: Playa Forum is a bustling beach that is close to Cancún's Hotel Zone and is well-known for its vivacious energy. It serves as a hub for socializing with other travelers and attending beach parties and water sports. Playa Forum is the ideal location for anyone seeking a balance of rest and excitement with its clean waters and vibrant atmosphere.
- ❖ The Caracol Playa: Since Playa Caracol has calm waves and shallow water, families frequently go there to take their kids somewhere fun and secure. The beach offers a variety of water sports, such as kayaking and paddleboarding, to

make sure that everyone can enjoy themselves in the sunshine.

- ❖ **Chac Mool Playa:** Playa Chac Mool is ideally situated and provides a variety of beach services and amenities. It is surrounded by hotels and resorts. It's simple to spend an entire day basking in the sun and taking in the seaside breeze thanks to the availability of sun loungers, umbrellas, and coastal eateries.
- ❖ **Performa Marlin:** Playa Marlin is a sanctuary for thrill-seekers and water sports lovers. Activities like parasailing, jet skiing, and banana boat excursions are ideal for this beach. A thrilling and unforgettable experience is created by the adrenaline rush and the breathtaking views.
- ❖ **Langosta Playa:** Playa Langosta is a calm beach with calm waves that is

perfect for swimming and snorkeling. Both locals and travelers looking for a tranquil escape frequently choose it because of its laid-back atmosphere and proximity to several hotels.

- ❖ **Juvenile Beach:** Playa Juventud, also referred to as "Youth Beach," is a favorite among locals and younger people. The lively environment, beach volleyball courts, and beachside pubs make it the perfect place for hanging out and having a good time with friends.

The beaches in Cancún are ideal for tourists looking for action, leisure, or a combination of the two. You can explore the wonders of nature, partake in adventurous pursuits, or just take in the beauty of the Mexican Caribbean's coastal riches because each beach offers its special charm.

Landmarks and Attractions You Must Visit

Cancún is full of must-see sights and attractions that will astound you with their natural beauty and rich cultural history. Here are some popular locations to check out while you're there:

- ❖ Archaeological Zone of El Rey: In the El Rey Archaeological Zone, where historic Mayan ruins are surrounded by beautiful vegetation, travel back in time. Investigate the impressively preserved structures and discover the fascinating past of this prehistoric culture.
- ❖ Underwater Museum of Cancún (MUSA): Explore the fascinating Cancún Underwater Museum by diving or snorkeling in the turquoise seas, where more than 500 sculptures are

submerged. This unusual gallery combines the beauty of the water with art to create an otherworldly experience.

- Isle of Contoy: Take a day excursion to the protected natural reserve and bird sanctuary known as Isla Contoy. Snorkel in the crystal-clear waters to find thriving marine life while admiring the beautiful range of flora and fauna on the island.
- Isle of Women: A short ferry ride will take you to the picturesque island of Isla Mujeres, where you can find peace. Take a stroll through the charming neighborhoods, unwind on the stunning beaches, and take in the relaxed island atmosphere.
- Park Xcaret: Discover the wonders of Xcaret Park, a wonderland of eco-archaeology honoring the natural and cultural history of Mexico. Swim in

hidden rivers, take in breathtaking shows, and savor the diversity of Mexican traditions.

- ❖ In Chichen Itza: Travel to Chichen Itza, one of the New Seven Wonders of the World, for the day. Discover the intriguing astronomical expertise of the ancient Maya as you tour the magnificent pyramids, temples, and observatories.
- ❖ Park, Xel-Há: A water lover's paradise, Xel-Há Park offers zip-lining, river rafting, and snorkeling excursions. Enjoy a smorgasbord of delectable regional and international food while relaxing in natural cenotes.
- ❖ Lake Nichupte: Discover the tranquil Nichupte Lagoon, a vast body of water that provides chances for kayaking, boat cruises, and birdwatching. This well-kept

secret offers a tranquil retreat from the busy city.

- ❖ Cancún's Interactive Aquarium: Experience marine life up close and personal at the Interactive Aquarium in Cancún. Engage in dolphin interactions, shark swimming, and enthralling marine displays to make lifelong memories for all ages.
- ❖ Beautiful Tower Enjoy breathtaking views of Cancún and the surrounding blue waters from the Scenic Tower, which offers a 360-degree panoramic. The observation deck offers a fantastic vantage point for taking beautiful pictures.

Cancún's sights and attractions guarantee a varied and enriching experience, with everything from ancient ruins to undersea wonders and tranquil natural reserves.

Copyrighted material

Chapter 3: The Wonders of the Riviera Maya

The Riviera Maya is a mesmerizing location that mesmerizes tourists with its stunning natural surroundings and extensive cultural history. Let's investigate the wonders this tropical haven has to offer:

Copyrighted material

Discovering Ancient Mayan Ruins and Archaeological Sites

The Riviera Maya is home to numerous Mayan archaeological monuments and ruins, each of which tells the tale of a fascinating civilization that once flourished there. Making your way back in time to these historical wonders is an amazing journey:

- ❖ Tulum: Tulum, perched on a clifftop with a view of the Caribbean Sea's turquoise waters, is a breathtaking example of the creativity of the Mayan civilization. Investigate the well-preserved buildings, such as El Castillo and the Temple of the Frescoes, which are covered in historic murals showing Mayan deities and celestial occasions.
- ❖ In Chichen Itza: Chichen Itza, one of the most famous archaeological sites in the

world, is a spellbinding example of Mayan architectural genius. Admire the magnificent Kukulkan Pyramid, an astronomical wonder that creates the well-known serpent-shadow descent by aligning with the equinoxes.

❖ Coba: Coba, a magical location hidden in the bush, beckons you to explore the cobblestone streets of the long-gone city. The tallest pyramid in the Yucatán can be climbed for panoramic views of the lush green canopy. It is called Nohoch Mul.

❖ in Ek Balam: Find out what makes Ek Balam, a little-known jewel with elaborate stucco sculptures and well-preserved structures, so special. Admire the impressive Acropolis, which serves as the gateway to the underworld, and be in awe of the skilled workmanship of the ancient craftspeople.

- Muyil: Muyil offers a peaceful location to explore the ruins surrounded by abundant flora and fauna because it is tucked away in the quiet Sian Ka'an Biosphere Reserve. Take a stroll down the historic sacbeob (white roads) and take in the peace of this less-frequented location.
- Nohoch Mul Temple of Coba: The Mayan ruins along the Riviera Maya provide an enthralling look into the sophisticated civilization's cosmological understanding, religious practices, and building prowess. These historic locations serve as evidence of the Mayans' close ties to nature and the cosmos.

Discovering the prehistoric Mayan ruins and archaeological sites of the Riviera Maya is a voyage through time and a chance to interact with an intriguing culture that had a profound impact on the history of the area. You will be in awe of the majesty and mystery of these locations, and the tales they reveal will stay with you long after you have left this extraordinary country.

Embracing Nature: Eco Parks, Cenotes, and Wildlife Reserves

Indulge in a world of eco-parks, cenotes, and wildlife reserves that celebrate the Riviera Maya's biodiversity and natural beauties by embracing nature there. Here's a closer look at the adventures you can expect:

- ❖ environmental Parks: The most well-known environmental parks in the Riviera Maya are Xcaret and Xel-Há. Xcaret offers underground rivers, animal encounters, and engaging shows. It is an intriguing fusion of ecological protection and cultural history. While snorkeling in freshwater rivers and cenotes in Xel-Há, you will be surrounded by lush flora and an abundance of marine life.

- ❖ Cenotes: The ancient Maya revered cenotes, which are natural sinkholes with crystal-clear pools, as sacred places, all around the Riviera Maya. Feel a deep connection to nature as you snorkel or swim in these alluring cenotes, like Dos Ojos, Gran Cenote, and Ik Kil.
- ❖ A UNESCO World Heritage site, the Sian Ka'an Biosphere Reserve is a vast wilderness where the land meets the sea. View a variety of bird species, dolphins, manatees, and even jaguars in their natural habitat as you explore mangroves, lagoons, and pristine beaches.

- ❖ Aktun Chen: Explore an underground cave network decorated with beautiful stalactites and stalagmites by entering the Aktun Chen natural park. The magnificence of the jungle canopy can be seen when strolling along the nature trails or from a treetop suspension bridge.
- ❖ The Akumal Sea Turtle Sanctuary is renowned for allowing visitors to snorkel alongside these docile animals in their natural habitat. It is very amazing to see sea turtles glide through the water with grace.
- ❖ Visit the Croco Cun Zoo to get up close and personal with local creatures and learn about conservation initiatives. For instructive and enjoyable experiences, people of all ages can engage with

crocodiles, monkeys, deer, and other local species at this interactive zoo.

- ❖ Rio Secreto: Rio Secreto is a bizarre world of stalactites and stalagmites that have been building for millions of years. Set off on an underground river journey here. You can take a guided tour of this eco-park to learn more about the geological past of the cave system.
- ❖ Isla Contoy, a pristine island, and protected nature reserve, is where you may view a huge variety of bird species and go snorkeling in waters filled with marine life.

In the Riviera Maya, embracing nature offers a strong connection to the environment and the chance to experience the ecological richness of the area.

Enjoying Peace in Calm Beaches and Coastal Towns

The Riviera Maya offers a tranquil retreat from the busy world with its calm beaches and coastal communities. Here are some lovely locations where you may relax and take in the laid-back atmosphere:

- ❖ Akumal: Akumal, a lovely coastal town known as the "Place of Turtles," is well-known for its sea turtle sanctuary. On its serene beaches, you may unwind and, if you're lucky, witness turtles swimming nearby. In a tranquil environment, snorkeling at Akumal Bay provides the chance to see colorful marine life.
- ❖ Tomás Morelos: Explore the charming fishing community of Puerto Morelos, a calm retreat only a short drive from

Cancun. Enjoy excellent seafood at beachside eateries while strolling along the beach and admiring the famous leaning lighthouse.

- ❖ Paraiso Playa: Playa Paraiso (Paradise Beach), as the name says, truly is a piece of paradise. This remote section of the beach has a calm environment that makes it perfect for reading a book or simply taking in the captivating Caribbean Sea.
- ❖ Beach Maroma: Escape to Playa Maroma, one of the most stunning beaches on earth. With its silky white dunes, calm surf, and tranquil atmosphere, this hidden gem is ideal for a day of delightful relaxation.
- ❖ Tijuana Beach: The beaches of Tulum have a bohemian ambiance that beckons you to relax and commune with nature.

Take advantage of the eco-chic beach clubs where you can relax in hammocks and sip cool drinks while taking in the mesmerizing ocean views.

- ❖ Xpu-Ha: You may enjoy the calm and tranquility of its undeveloped beaches in the tranquil paradise of Xpu-Ha. Pure calm can be attained by strolling down the coastline while hearing the quiet waves and sensing the spongy sand beneath your feet.
- ❖ Punta Esmeralda Playa: Visit Playa Punta Esmeralda in Playa del Carmen for a local favorite. This beach is well-known for its laid-back vibe, its calm waters, and the surrounding cenote (natural pool), where you may cool off and take in the beauty of nature.
- ❖ Bay of Soliman: Soliman Bay is a serene haven away from tourists since it is

remote and idyllic. This beach is the perfect location for beachcombing, sunbathing, and admiring the splendor of an undeveloped Caribbean coastline because it is surrounded by rich vegetation.

Enjoying quiet at the Riviera Maya's calm beaches and coastal communities is a chance to relax and rejuvenate amidst the beauty of nature. Whether you're looking for a quiet retreat or a relaxed atmosphere, these serene havens guarantee a calming experience that will leave you feeling renewed and invigorated.

Copyrighted material

Chapter 4: Outdoor Activities and Adventure

The Riviera Maya is a haven for thrill-seekers, offering a wide variety of exhilarating outdoor pursuits that will satisfy any adrenaline junkie. Prepare to set out on adventurous journeys and make priceless memories:

47|Glasgow Traveler's Handbook

Copyrighted material

Aquatic Adventures and Exciting Water Sports

For those looking for adrenaline-pumping experiences in the Caribbean Sea's beautiful waters, the Riviera Maya offers a wide variety of thrilling water sports and aquatic excursions. Add the following thrilling activities to your bucket list:

- ❖ Subaquatic diving: Dive beneath the surface to explore a coral reef paradise brimming with aquatic life. There are many top-notch diving locations in the Riviera Maya, like the Mamita's Reef in Playa del Carmen and the Palancar Reef on Cozumel, where you may see beautiful sea turtles, schools of tropical fish, and even nurse sharks.
- ❖ Snorkeling: You can explore the marine beauties from the surface while

snorkeling for a more relaxed but no less intriguing experience. Explore vibrant coral formations and tropical fish in the shallow bays and cenotes that are shielded from the elements.

- ❖ a jet ski: As you ride a jet ski across the azure waves, feel the surge of exhilaration. A thrilling way to explore the coastline is via jet skiing, which provides expansive views of the Caribbean Sea and a feeling of freedom on the waves.
- ❖ Parasailing: Fly over the water to see the breathtaking beaches of the Riviera Maya from above. With the thrilling activity of parasailing, you may soar above the water and enjoy beautiful views of the coastline and the great ocean.
- ❖ Kayaking: On a kayaking expedition, paddle through tranquil mangroves and

discover secret lagoons. Kayaking provides an opportunity to go close to nature, see local wildlife up close, and enjoy the serene beauty of the area's natural environments.

- ❖ Flyboarding: Flyboarding is an exhilarating water sport that uses high-pressure water jets to lift you into the air so you may get the sensation of flight. As you hover over the water's surface and experience a sense of superhuman strength, test your agility and balance.
- ❖ Kiteboarding: Use kiteboarding to ride the waves and harness the strength of the wind. The consistent trade winds in the Riviera Maya make it the perfect location for this thrilling sport, giving fans of water sports an adrenaline-pumping experience.

❖ Diver Snuba: Snuba diving provides the ideal answer for individuals who want to explore the depths without needing a scuba certification. Snuba enables you to explore spectacular coral formations and marine life while breathing underwater using a unique device.

Every level of thrill seeker can enjoy the exhilarating water sports and aquatic experiences offered in the Riviera Maya, from diving into the depths to soaring above the water.

Exploring the Lush Jungles and Zip-Lining through Nature

Entering the Riviera Maya's luxuriant jungles is a gateway to exhilarating encounters that connect you with the beauty of nature. What awaits you in this lush wonderland is as follows:

- ❖ Zip-Lining: An adventure filled with adrenaline awaits you as you soar through the jungle canopy on thrilling zip lines. Enjoy the wind's rush over your face while seeing the amazing vistas of the lush vegetation below. A must-try activity that mixes adventure and the peace of the outdoors is zip-lining.
- ❖ Off-Road ATV Adventures: Off-road ATV trips allow you to travel through rocky terrain and thick vegetation. Discover hidden cenotes and historic sites as you navigate across muddy trails and travel further into the bush.
- ❖ Forest Hiking: Put on your hiking boots and go for a stroll in the beautiful jungle pathways. Investigate various ecosystems, look for local wildlife, and take in the air's avian orchestra.

- ❖ Cenote investigation: Learn about cenotes, which are naturally occurring sinkholes with crystal-clear water. After an active day, certain cenotes provide a pleasant refuge where you may swim and cool off.
- ❖ Treetop Walks: Enjoy the thrill of walking among the trees on canopy walks and suspension bridges. These elevated trails provide you with a special vantage point on the biodiversity of the forest and allow you to have a closer look at the local flora and fauna.
- ❖ Birdwatching: As home to a wide variety of vibrant avian species, the rainforests of the Riviera Maya are a sanctuary for birdwatchers. Take out your binoculars and scan the treetops for toucans, parrots, and other intriguing species.

- ❖ Eco parks and nature reserves: Visit environmental parks and nature reserves devoted to conserving the natural beauty of the Riviera Maya. These protected areas have educated guides who share insights into the ecology of the jungle and conservation initiatives on guided tours.
- ❖ Jungle Ruins from the Past: Some historical places are tucked away in the woods, away from prying eyes. Investigate these historic sites, such as Muyil and Coba, and try to picture how the Mayan civilization, which once flourished amidst the lush vegetation, lived.

Discovering the Riviera Maya's lush rainforests is an immersive experience that lets you get close to the beauties of nature. Among the thrilling adventures that lie ahead are hiking via secret routes, zip-lining through the treetops, and discovering cenotes.

Scuba and Snorkeling in the Caribbean Sea: A Diver's Paradise

You can enter a world of amazing undersea delights by scuba diving in the Caribbean Sea. The Riviera Maya provides a variety of scuba and snorkeling thrills, whether you're an experienced diver or a novice:

Subaquatic diving:

- ❖ Reefs: The Riviera Maya is home to a complex web of coral reefs that are teaming with marine life. Visit places like Cozumel's Palancar Reef, where beautiful coral formations provide as a colorful backdrop for encounters with sea turtles, nurse sharks, and schools of tropical fish.

- ❖ Cenotes: Learn about the mystique of cenote diving, a singular experience that allows you to enter freshwater sinkholes beneath the surface. Dos Ojos and The Pit cenotes both have intriguing rock formations and unearthly scenery.
- ❖ Wrecks: The Caribbean Sea is home to undiscovered riches for wreck divers. Discover sunken ships that offer a peek into history and attract marine life, such as the C-56, a former navy minesweeper, and the Mama Via.

Visit up close and personal with a wide variety of aquatic animals. Admire the majestic rays' majesty, nurse sharks' inquisitiveness, and the lively antics of tropical fish schools.

Snorkeling:

- **Coral Gardens:** Snorkel in the shallow water above the coral gardens to take in the reef's splendor up close. Excellent snorkeling locations with a diversity of marine life may be found at Akumal's Yal-Ku Lagoon and Puerto Morelos' National Marine Park.
- **Sea turtles:** While snorkeling in Akumal Bay, you can see friendly sea turtles in their natural habitat. These gorgeous creatures create a magical and unforgettable experience as they flow gently through the water.
- **Cenotes:** Snorkeling provides a unique perspective of the magnificent rock formations within the cenote as well as the hypnotic play of light within the underwater tunnels. Many cenotes are accessible for snorkeling.

❖ Shore snorkeling in Cozumel: The west coast of Cozumel offers options for shore snorkeling. Popular locations where you may readily examine marine life just a few steps from the water's edge include El Cielo and Palancar Beach.

The Caribbean Sea offers insights into a fascinating underwater world teeming with life and beauty through scuba diving and snorkeling. These aquatic activities promise unique pleasures for nature lovers and water lovers alike, whether you're exploring bright coral reefs, swimming with sea turtles, or discovering the mystical cenotes.

Copyrighted material

Chapter 5: Indulging in Mexican Caribbean Flavors

The Mexican Caribbean is a culinary haven with mouthwateringly rich flavors and a wide variety of cuisine. Here is a mouthwatering tour of the area's culinary attractions:

Copyrighted material

Mexican Cuisine: A Gastronomic Tour

A culinary adventure through Mexican food is a delight for the senses. The Mexican Caribbean offers a diverse tapestry of flavors that convey the tale of a rich culinary tradition, from the streets of lively markets to the exquisite dining rooms of upmarket restaurants.

Start your exploration with the dishes that have come to represent Mexican cuisine. Tacos are a must-try because they have soft tortillas stuffed with flavorful meats, fresh salsa, and vivid toppings. Tacos made with juicy al pastor or delicate barbacoa will tempt your palate with each bite.

Another hallmark of Mexican cuisine is enchiladas, which feature wrapped tortillas slathered in a variety of mouthwatering sauces. Each region has its variation of this well-liked dish, from the acidic tomatillo sauce to the luscious mole.

Discover the flavors of cochinita pibil, a typical meal made of tender, slow-roasted pork marinated in achiote paste and citrus liquids, by exploring the culinary history of the Yucatán Peninsula. For a flavor explosion, serve it with pickled onions and wrap it in a warm tortilla.

Those who enjoy seafood will be delighted by the plentiful fresh catches from the Caribbean Sea. The acidic and salty tastes of ceviche, a light dish of marinated fish or shrimp in citrus juices, are well balanced. Consume camarones al ajillo, shrimp sautéed in oil flavored with garlic, for a sumptuous feast.

The Mexican Caribbean offers a variety of energizing drinks to go with your meal. Drink some horchata, a sweet beverage made from rice that has cinnamon and vanilla flavors, or agua de Jamaica, a colorful infusion of hibiscus flowers.

Continue your culinary adventure by visiting food markets, where the perfume of freshly ground spices and sizzling delicacies fills the air. Try some antojitos, a variety of delectable street foods like empanadas, quesadillas, and elotes (Mexican street corn), each with a distinctive flavor profile.

A sweet end to a Mexican supper is also required. Churros, a crunchy fried dough treat covered in cinnamon sugar, or flan, a smooth caramel custard that melts on your tongue will satisfy your sweet craving.

Mexican cuisine in the Caribbean is a celebration of varied flavors and cultural influences, ranging from the straightforwardness of street food to the complexity of regional delicacies.

Best Restaurants, Food Markets, and Street Eats

The Mexican Caribbean offers a wide variety of eating alternatives to satisfy every taste and budget when it comes to culinary delights. Here are some places where you may sample the region's best flavors, from little food markets to fancy restaurants and busy street food:

Food stores:

Experience the heart of Mexican cuisine by immersing yourself in the lively ambiance of neighborhood food markets. Here, you may sample a range of traditional delicacies. In Cancun, Mercado 28 is a well-liked location to enjoy regional specialties, including delectable tacos and recently caught seafood. Calle 38 in Playa del Carmen is a relaxed beachfront market where you can indulge in delectable ceviche and other seafood treats.

Copyrighted material

High-end restaurants:

The Mexican Caribbean region offers a wide variety of luxury restaurants that highlight the best flavors of the area for a refined dining experience. Discover the culinary innovations of renowned chefs that combine modern cooking methods with traditional Mexican ingredients. These restaurants offer a sophisticated voyage across the area's culinary scene, from stylish coastal businesses to sumptuous dining rooms.

Street Food:

The delicious odors of street food vendors fill the streets of the Mexican Caribbean. Try the well-known street tacos, where you may add a variety of fresh toppings and salsas to customize the contents. Another popular street dish is elotes (Mexican street corn), which is grilled corn topped with mayo, cheese, and chili powder.

Beachfront Restaurants:

You can find wonderful seaside restaurants that combine foreign flavors with regional ingredients as you meander along the coast. Enjoy fresh ceviche, tropical fruit cocktails, and seafood platters while taking in the Caribbean Sea's beautiful vistas and the sea wind.

Specialties of the Region:

There are gastronomic gems to be found in every part of the Mexican Caribbean. Enjoy the flavors of panuchos, cochinita pibil, and pollo pibil in the Yucatán Peninsula. Try the seafood specialties in Cozumel, such as tikin-xic, a typical Mayan fish dish prepared with achiote and tart citrus. Get a taste of the lobster pizza, Isla Mujeres's famous delicacy.

The dining scene in the Mexican Caribbean is a fascinating combination of tastes and influences that highlights the area's extensive culinary history. Each dining experience promises to be a one-of-a-kind and spectacular culinary journey, whether you choose to peruse bustling food markets, taste a gourmet dinner at a chic restaurant, or indulge in the local street cuisine.

Indulging in Regional Delicacies and Refreshing Beverages

A great feast for the senses is having local cuisine and cool drinks in the Mexican Caribbean. Here is what you really must sample throughout your culinary adventure, from traditional dishes that celebrate local flavors to thirst-quenching beverages that battle the heat:

Local specialties:

- ❖ Cochinita Pibil: This mouthwatering Yucatecan specialty is slow-roasted pork that has been marinated in achiote paste and citrus liquids. Cochinita pibil, which is served with pickled onions and wrapped in warm tortillas, is a taste explosion that encapsulates the spirit of the area.

- ❖ Salbutes: A favorite Yucatecan street meal, these crisp tortillas are topped with shredded chicken, avocado, lettuce, and pickled onions. Salbutes are a delicious treat for your taste buds because of the combination of textures and flavors.
- ❖ Papadzules: A special Yucatán Peninsula meal, papadzules consists of tortillas stuffed with hard-boiled eggs and topped with a mouthwatering pumpkin seed sauce. Food lovers should try this flavorful and warming dish.
- ❖ Seafood Ceviche: Due to the availability of fresh catches from the Caribbean Sea, seafood ceviche is a well-liked option. This meal, which is marinated in citrus juices and combined with chopped

onions, tomatoes, and cilantro, is delicious on a hot day.

- ❖ Tamales: Steamed maize dough loaded with a variety of savory or sweet fillings is a classic of Mexican cuisine. Enjoy the flavor of traditional tamales made with chicken or pig or try something new like mole or pineapple sweetness.

energizing drinks:

- ❖ Agua de Jamaica: This colorful hibiscus flower beverage is visually beautiful as well as pleasant. It offers a nice combination of flowery and tangy aromas and is lightly sweetened with sugar.
- ❖ Horchata: This well-known beverage made from rice is scented with cinnamon and vanilla and is creamy and slightly sweet, making it ideal for cooling off.
- ❖ Tamarind Water: Made from tamarind pods, this sweetened, somewhat tangy

beverage is frequently served over ice. A distinctive and tasty beverage choice is tamarind water.

- ❖ Margarita: The traditional margarita is a must-try when it comes to cocktails. A Mexican Caribbean staple, this delightful beverage is made with tequila, triple sec, and fresh lime juice.
- ❖ The michelada is a tangy and fiery beer-based cocktail made with lime juice, hot sauce, and various ingredients. Ideal for adding a little twist to a chilled beer.

The Mexican Caribbean experience is not complete without indulging in local cuisine and drinking cool beverages. Each gastronomic delicacy is a reflection of the region's cultural past and various influences, from the flavors of cochinita pibil and papadzules to the exquisite aguas frescas and distinctive cocktails.

Copyrighted material

Chapter 6: Useful Preparation for a Memorable Trip

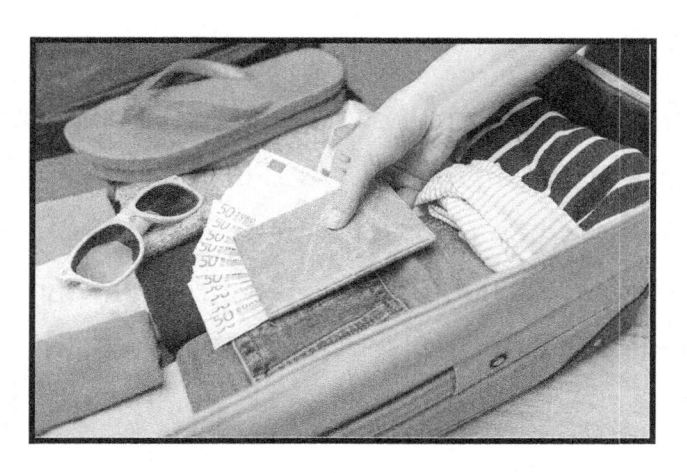

Practical planning goes a long way when preparing for an amazing trip to the Mexican Caribbean. Here are some crucial pointers to make sure you have a hassle-free and pleasurable trip:

Choosing the Right Accommodations: Resorts, Hotels, and Rentals

You have a variety of options to choose from that can accommodate various tastes and price ranges when it comes to lodging for your Mexican Caribbean excursion. The primary kinds of lodging are broken down as follows:

- ❖ Resorts: All-inclusive resorts in the Mexican Caribbean provide all you need for a comfortable and enjoyable stay. Resorts are ideal for individuals looking for a stress-free vacation because they offer a variety of amenities like several eating options, pools, spas, and entertainment. You can choose between resorts that cater to families with kids' clubs and water parks or adults-only getaways with an emphasis on luxury and relaxation.

- ❖ Hotels: There are many different types and sizes of hotels in the Mexican Caribbean, ranging from beachside boutique hotels to well-known multinational brands. Hotels are a wonderful option if you value freedom and flexibility throughout your visit. They provide cozy lodging, on-site dining, and frequently easy access to neighboring activities and attractions.
- ❖ Rentals for holidays: Vacation rentals are a great choice for vacationers looking for a home-like setting. Private villas, condos, and seaside homes are all readily accessible for short-term rentals. For families or groups of friends, vacation rentals are ideal because they provide

lots of space, fully functional kitchens, and the flexibility to set your schedule.

Factors to Bear in Mind:

Location: Think about how the location of your accommodations fits with your travel schedule. Beachfront hotels have breathtaking views of the ocean and quick access to the sand, whereas hotels in towns may be closer to the town's bars, restaurants, and stores.

Accommodations: Look for lodgings that offer the features you want. Making the correct amenities selections improves your total holiday experience, whether it's a spa for relaxation, a fitness center for workouts, or on-site restaurants with a variety of dining alternatives.

Budget: Establish a spending limit and look for lodging that fits it. Recall that some all-inclusive resorts include meals and entertainment, which might make it easier for you to budget and control your spending.

Copyrighted material

Reviews: To learn more about the caliber of the accommodations and services provided, read reviews left by past visitors. Online review sites can offer insightful commentary from actual travelers.

Special Offers: Keep an eye out for special offers and promotions, especially during off-peak times, since they might help you land enticing discounts or extra benefits.

The ideal lodgings for your Mexican Caribbean journey will ultimately rely on your interests, travel style, and the experiences you hope to have while there. Your accommodations, whether you pick an opulent beachfront resort, a quaint boutique hotel, or a comfortable vacation rental, will serve as the foundation for your lifelong memories of this tropical paradise.

Navigating Transportation and Getting Around the Area

The Mexican Caribbean offers simple transportation options that can be tailored to your preferences. Here is a map to help you navigate the area with ease:

- ❖ Renting a vehicle: If you want the flexibility to travel to various locations at your speed, renting a car is a great option. Rental car companies are easily accessible at airports and in well-known tourist locations. Make sure your driver's license is up to date, and for a piece of mind, think about getting insurance. Road journeys are enjoyable because of the region's well-kept motorways, and you can quickly reach surrounding sites and undiscovered jewels.

- ❖ Regional Transport: For moving about cities and towns, convenient options include taxis and colectivos (shared vans). There are taxis available at hotels, airports, and popular tourist destinations, and many of them have set fares for particular routes. On the other hand, colectivos have predetermined itineraries and can be flagged down by the side of the road. They let you interact with locals while traveling and are an affordable choice for short distances.
- ❖ Commuter Buses: In the Mexican Caribbean, public buses provide an affordable means to get between towns and cities. Coaches that are cozy and air-conditioned are available from ADO and other bus companies regularly. Popular attractions are connected by

these buses, making it simple to explore the area without the burden of a car.

- ❖ **Cycling rentals:** Consider hiring a bicycle for an enjoyable and environmentally beneficial way to travel. Many tourist destinations offer bike rental options, enabling you to leisurely cruise along seaside roads or explore the towns. Cycling is a fun way to stay active while taking in the area's picturesque scenery.
- ❖ **Ferries to Adjacent Islands:** Ferries offer practical transportation for day trips to adjacent islands like Cozumel or Isla Mujeres. From specific ports, ferries run, and the trip provides breathtaking views of the Caribbean Sea. Make sure to review the ferry timetable before setting off on your day trip.
- ❖ **Walking:** Walking is a practical and entertaining way to explore many tourist

places. Explore hidden jewels on foot as you meander through colorful alleyways and along beachfront promenades. You may immerse yourself in the local culture and discover quaint cafés, stores, and street art by walking.

Getting Around Advice:

- ❖ Carry Tiny Bills: Keep Mexican pesos in tiny denominations on hand for small purchases like taxi fares.
- ❖ Plan by researching your alternatives for getting there before you go so you know what to anticipate.
- ❖ Embrace Adventure: Be open to attempting new forms of transportation as exploring the area's transportation alternatives may be an adventure in and of itself.

One of the exciting parts of your tour will be figuring out the transportation system in the

Mexican Caribbean. Each method of transportation offers different sensations, whether you're traveling along picturesque coastline roads, boarding a local colectivo, or strolling through energetic town centers.

Tips for Safety and Health for a Worry-Free Vacation

With this safety advice and health measures, you can have a worry-free trip to the Mexican Caribbean:

- ❖ Personal Property: Be careful with your valuables, especially in crowded places and popular tourist destinations. Your passport, wallet, and phone should be carried in a money belt or a safe crossbody purse. Displaying pricey jewelry or electronics that can draw unwanted attention is not a good idea.

- ❖ Using Sunscreen: The Mexican Caribbean has plenty of sunshine, so shield your eyes from the harmful rays by donning sunglasses, a wide-brimmed hat, and sunscreen with a high SPF. Drink plenty of water throughout the day to stay hydrated, especially if you're out sightseeing or at the beach.
- ❖ Swimming Safety: Swimming in the open water requires caution because the currents can be powerful. Swimming should only be done in places where lifeguards are on duty. If you're thinking about participating in water sports like diving or snorkeling, pick trustworthy companies with trained guides.
- ❖ Warnings for your health: Before you leave, make sure your usual vaccines are current by speaking with your doctor. Hepatitis A and typhoid vaccinations

should be taken into consideration as they may be advised for travel to the area. If you have any particular health issues, make sure you have the essential prescriptions and a first aid kit with you.

- ❖ Water and Food: Although the Mexican Caribbean has some excellent restaurants, be careful where and what you eat. Reputable eateries and street food vendors with respectable cleanliness standards are preferred. Avoid eating foods that are uncooked or undercooked, and only consume purified or bottled water from reliable sources.
- ❖ Observe regional customs: To respect the local community, become familiar with cultural norms and customs. An uncomplicated "hola" and a grin go a long way in Mexico because greetings are frequently cordial and welcoming.

Respect local customs by adhering to rules and dressing modestly when visiting holy places or nearby villages.

❖ Contact information for emergencies: Keep important contact information handy, such as the local embassy or consulate of your nation. Additionally, it's a good idea to store the phone numbers for the local emergency services and your lodging on your phone.

❖ Climate Readiness: Pay attention to weather forecasts, especially from June through November when hurricanes are expected. Although hurricanes are uncommon in the Mexican Caribbean, it is still advisable to keep informed and heed local advice if there are any weather-related issues while you are there.

Copyrighted material

You can have a worry-free trip to the Mexican Caribbean by paying attention to this safety advice and health precautions. During your stay in this enchanted paradise, embrace the area's beauty, acquaint yourself with the local culture, and make lasting memories.

Copyrighted material

Chapter 7: Beyond Cancun & The Riviera Maya

Exploring the world outside of Cancun and the Riviera Maya gives up a world of interesting experiences and undiscovered jewels. Consider the following amazing locations and activities for an unforgettable adventure:

Day Trips to Nearby Islands and Charming Coastal Towns

From Cancun and the Riviera Maya, day visits to adjacent islands and quaint coastal towns bring up a world of exploration and adventure. Consider the following amazing locations for a day vacation to remember:

- ❖ Cozumel: Take a ferry from Playa del Carmen to the diving and snorkeling haven of Cozumel. Discover the spectacular coral reefs on the island, which are teaming up with vibrant marine life. For a chance to swim with dolphins or just to unwind on the gorgeous beaches, head to Chankanaab National Park.
- ❖ Isle of Women: Take a ferry to the peaceful island of Isla Mujeres, which is renowned for its relaxed attitude and

gorgeous beaches. Rent a golf cart to discover the island's undiscovered beauties, go snorkeling in the pristine waters, and don't skip the chance to see the charming Punta Sur.

- ❖ Isle of Holbox: Visit the tranquil and free-spirited island of Isla Holbox, which is off the Yucatán Peninsula's northern shore. Observe the enchanted "bioluminescence" phenomena at night and take in the serenity of this idyllic island setting.
- ❖ Tomás Morelos: Discover Puerto Morelos' beauty, a sleepy fishing community located between Cancun and Playa del Carmen. Swim or snorkel at the Mesoamerican Barrier Reef System, the second-largest reef system in the world, which includes the Puerto Morelos Reef National Park.

- ❖ Akumal: Go to Akumal, a tiny seaside settlement renowned for its lovely bay and sea turtle population. Enjoy Akumal's beaches' natural beauty while snorkeling among these friendly critters.
- ❖ Puerto Morelos: Discover the bustling streets of Playa del Carmen, a lively coastal town. Quinta Avenida (Fifth Avenue) is a great place to people-watch while you shop and eat. Spend the day relaxing and having fun at the beach clubs and restaurants that are right on the sand.
- ❖ Tulum: Visit Tulum, which is renowned for its intact Mayan ruins that gaze out over the Caribbean Sea. After seeing the historic city, have a refreshing dip and enjoy the stunning scenery at the adjacent beach.

❖ **Bacalar:** The charming "Lake of Seven Colors" may be found in Bacalar, a little community south of the Riviera Maya. Swim in the clear waters and take a boat tour to see the lake's many colors of blue that give it its captivating appearance.

Day tours to these surrounding islands and coastal communities provide a variety of experiences, from cultural explorations to undersea adventures.

Every place has its distinct attraction and charm, promising a day full of life-enriching experiences and memories.

Exploring the Yucatán Peninsula's Hidden Gems

Discovering the hidden gems of the Yucatán Peninsula opens up a world of wonders rich in history and breathtaking scenery. Here are some fascinating places to include on your travel itinerary:

- ❖ In Chichen Itza: Learn about the magnificent Chichen Itza ruins, which are the remains of a former Mayan metropolis and a UNESCO World Heritage Site. Admire the famous El Castillo pyramid, the Temple of the Warriors, and the El Caracol astronomy observatory. Chichen Itza is a must-visit location because of its extensive history and magnificent architecture.
- ❖ Cenotes: There are many cenotes, or natural sinkholes created by collapsing limestone, on the Yucatán Peninsula. These cenotes invite you to swim in their crystal-clear waters or snorkel through underwater caves decorated with stalactites and stalagmites for a surreal experience. Cenotes like Ik Kil, Cenote

Dos Ojos, and Cenote Suytun shouldn't be missed.

- ❖ **Uxmal:** Visit the historic ruins at Uxmal, a noteworthy additional Mayan archaeological site. The Governor's Palace, the Nunnery Quadrangle, and the Pyramid of the Magician are examples of Mayan architectural expertise and offer insight into the intricate rites and beliefs of the society.
- ❖ **Izamal:** Izamal, also referred to as the "Yellow City," is a lovely town with colonial-style buildings and a strong Maya tradition. A horse-drawn carriage ride through the charming alleyways and a visit to the spectacular Franciscan Monastery, which was constructed atop a pre-Hispanic pyramid, are both highly recommended.

- Valladolid: Discover Valladolid's colonial charm, a small town with colorful structures and a lively central square. Visit the magnificent San Gervasio Cathedral, cool down in the neighboring Cenote Zaci, and dine at neighborhood restaurants serving delectable Yucatecan food.
- in Ek Balam: Explore the historic ruins at Ek Balam, an archeological site that is still uncovering buried riches. Explore the beautifully adorned buildings of the Acropolis and climb its towering entrance arch, known as the Jaguar Mouth, for panoramic views.
- The Rio Lagartos: The seaside fishing community of Rio Lagartos, which is alive with biodiversity, set off on a wildlife expedition. Visit the Ra Lagartos Biosphere Reserve by boat to see

flamingos, crocodiles, and numerous bird species in their natural surroundings.

- ❖ Coba: Visit Coba, a historic Maya city surrounded by a lush jungle, and travel back in time. To tour the expansive archaeological site, which features the Nohoch Mul pyramid, the tallest pyramid on the Yucatán Peninsula, you can rent a bicycle or rickshaw.

You can gain insights into the historic Maya civilization and have the opportunity to immerse yourself in breathtaking natural settings by exploring the Yucatán Peninsula's hidden beauties. Each hidden jewel guarantees a one-of-a-kind and never-to-be-forgotten experience, whether you're exploring historic ruins or swimming in enchanted cenotes.

Extending Your Adventure to Other Alluring Mexican Destinations

You may explore Mexico's varied landscapes, culture, and history by extending your adventure to other appealing locations. Consider including these fascinating locations on your travel itinerary:

- ❖ Mexican capital: Discover Mexico City, the country's vivacious capital and a center of culture and tradition. Explore famous sites including the historic district, the magnificent Zócalo Square, and the imposing Metropolitan Cathedral. At renowned museums like the National Museum of Anthropology and the Frida Kahlo Museum, immerse yourself in art and history.

- ❖ Guanajuato: Learn about Guanajuato, a magical city renowned for its vibrant colonial architecture and winding streets. The city's unusual tunnels can be explored, and the El Pipila Monument offers sweeping vistas. Don't forget to visit the intriguing mummy museum and the magnificent Teatro Juárez.
- ❖ Oaxaca: Discover the enchantment of Oaxaca, a place famed for its traditional arts and crafts, delectable cuisine, and cultural celebrations. Take a stroll through the vibrant marketplaces, see the historic ruins at Monte Albán, and savor the mouthwatering mole and mezcal flavors of Oaxacan cuisine.
- ❖ De Allende, San Miguel: Take in the artistic atmosphere of San Miguel de Allende, a colonial city bursting with art studios, galleries, and exquisitely

preserved architecture. Visit the neo-gothic Parroquia de San Miguel Arcángel and take in the lively arts and crafts market in the city's central square, El Jardn.

- ❖ Port of Mexico: Relax in Puerto Vallarta, a charming coastal town renowned for its breathtaking beaches and exciting nightlife. Travel by boat to the secluded beaches of Yelapa or Las Caletas, stroll along the picturesque Malecón boardwalk and take in the bustling ambiance of the Zona Romantica.
- ❖ Chiapas: Visit Chiapas, a place bursting with natural beauty and indigenous culture. Visit the historic ruins of Palenque, take a boat tour down the verdant Sumidero Canyon, and discover the indigenous settlements and

marketplaces in San Cristóbal de las Casas.

- ❖ Peninsula of Yucatán: Extend your trip to the Yucatán Peninsula and see lesser-known wonders like Valladolid, a lovely village, the azure waters of Bacalar's Lake of Seven Colors, and Ek Balam, a less-traveled Mayan ruin.
- ❖ Southern California: Discover Baja California's various landscapes, from the magnificent beaches of Los Cabos to the thriving wine region of Valle de Guadalupe. Explore the wild beauty of Sierra de San Pedro Mártir National Park or go whale watching in Loreto.

By extending your journey to further Mexican locations, you can learn more about the nation's rich cultural heritage, magnificent scenery, and friendly people.

Copyrighted material

Chapter 8: Helpful Resources and Information

Useful Information & Resources offers crucial information to make your trip to the Mexican Caribbean easier and more pleasurable. Here are some essential tools and pointers to have in mind:

Copyrighted material

Language Guide and Communication Tips

Navigating language in the Mexican Caribbean is made easy with these communication tips:

- ❖ Basic Spanish Phrases:
   While many locals speak English in tourist areas, knowing a few basic Spanish phrases can enhance your travel experience and show respect for the local culture. Learn greetings like "hola" (hello), "por favor" (please), and "gracias" (thank you). Simple expressions like "¿Cómo estás?" (How are you?) and "disculpe" (excuse me) will come in handy during your interactions.
- ❖ Polite Expressions:
   Mexican culture values politeness, so incorporating phrases like "Buenos días"

(good morning), "buenas trades" (good afternoon), and "buenas noches" (good evening) can make a positive impression. When addressing someone, use "señor" (sir) for men and "señora" (ma'am) for women.

- ❖ Smile and Gestures: Even if you're not fluent in Spanish, a warm smile and friendly demeanor can bridge language barriers. Non-verbal communication, like gestures and body language, can help convey your message and foster positive interactions.
- ❖ English-Friendly Places: In popular tourist areas, you'll find many establishments, such as hotels, restaurants, and shops, with English-speaking staff. However, embracing the local language can enrich

your experience and show a genuine interest in the culture.

- ❖ Language Apps and Translation Tools:
  If you need assistance with language translation, consider using language apps or translation tools on your smartphone. These handy tools can help you communicate effectively and provide quick translations on the go.
- ❖ Embrace the Learning Experience: Don't be afraid to try speaking Spanish, even if it's just a few words. Locals appreciate the effort, and practicing the language can lead to meaningful interactions and cultural exchange.
- ❖ Respectful Communication: Be patient and respectful when communicating with locals. Speak clearly and avoid raising your voice if there's a language barrier. Be open to asking for clarification and

repeating phrases to ensure understanding.
- ❖ **Learn About Local Customs:** Understanding local customs and cultural norms can enhance communication and prevent misunderstandings. For example, Mexicans are generally friendly and value personal connections, so engaging in small talk and being courteous is appreciated.

By embracing the language and communication tips, you can navigate the Mexican Caribbean with ease and connect with locals on a more personal level. Whether you're ordering delicious street food, bargaining at a market, or simply exchanging pleasantries, speaking a few words in Spanish will add a delightful touch to your travel experience.

Copyrighted material

Travelers' Money and Currency Issues

A good travel experience in the Mexican Caribbean requires careful consideration of currency and financial issues:

- ❖ Licensed Currency: The Mexican Peso (MXN) is the country of Mexico's official currency. To get a sense of how much the peso is worth in your home currency, it is best to become familiar with the current exchange rate before your trip.
- ❖ Cards and Cash: For your trip, pack a combination of cash and credit/debit cards. Smaller shops and local markets might prefer cash even though cards are generally accepted in tourist destinations and larger institutions. While ATMs are easily accessible in busy areas, choose

the ones inside reputed banks to avoid any potential surcharges.

- ❖ **Converting Money:** Avoid converting money at airports since the rates and costs are frequently higher and less beneficial. Use approved currency exchange offices or local banks instead for better rates.
- ❖ **Paying Customs:** In Mexico, especially in the service sector, tipping is customary. It's customary to tip between 10% and 15% of the whole cost when dining out. Rounding up the fee for other services, such as taxi trips or guided tours, is appreciated.
- ❖ **Expenses and budgeting:** Make a budget for your trip, taking into account lodging, food, travel, and activities. Although living prices might vary based on your choices and travel style, they are often less

expensive in the Mexican Caribbean than in many Western nations.

- ❖ **Safety measures:** Secure your goods and money. Use travel pouches or hotel safes to store your passport, critical papers, and extra cash. When handling cash in public, use caution to prevent attracting unwanted attention.
- ❖ **Dollar Abbreviations:** Learn about the various Peso banknotes and coin denominations used in Mexico. Coins range in value from 5 centavos to 10 pesos, while banknotes are available in denominations ranging from 20 to 1,000 pesos.
- ❖ **Tell Your Bank:** To avoid any problems using your credit/debit cards overseas, let your bank know before you leave about your travel dates and destination.

This will prevent them from mistaking your overseas transactions for fraud.

You may manage your spending easily and take a worry-free trip to the Mexican Caribbean by being prepared with knowledge about currencies and financial problems. To get the most out of your vacation experience, carry cash and credit cards sensibly, learn the etiquette surrounding tipping, and be aware of your spending limits.

List of Things to Pack and Travel Essentials

Making a packing list and making sure you have the necessary travel things can make your trip to the Mexican and Caribbean stress-free and pleasurable. What you should add is as follows:

- ❖ Clothing: Pack breathable, cozy clothes that are appropriate for warm temperatures. For days at the beach, pack t-shirts, shorts, sundresses, and swimwear. For chilly evenings, pack a lightweight jacket or sweater. Don't forget to bring a reusable water bottle, sunglasses, and a hat with a wide brim.
- ❖ Footwear: For beach and informal outings, pack a pair of sandals or flip-flops. When seeing historical sites or natural parks, it is best to wear comfortable walking shoes or sneakers. Consider bringing hiking or water shoes if you intend to trek or engage in other outdoor activities.
- ❖ Using Sunscreen: Use a sunscreen (SPF 30 or higher), lip balm with SPF, and after-sun lotion to shield yourself from the sun's rays. During beach days, a beach

umbrella or sun hat will provide additional shade.

- ❖ Travel papers: Your passport, license, and any required visas should all be kept in a safe travel pouch. Important documents should be copied and kept separately in case of emergency. Don't forget to include any necessary vaccination records and information about your travel insurance.
- ❖ Electronics and accessories: Bring your smartphone, camera, or GoPro with you so you can document your adventure. Bring adapters, power banks, and chargers that are compatible with Mexican power outlets.
- ❖ A first aid kit including medications: Bring along any required personal medications, prescription drugs, and a basic first aid kit

107|Glasgow Traveler's Handbook

with adhesive bandages, antiseptic wipes, pain relievers, and other supplies.

- ❖ **Toiletries for travel:** Bring travel-sized items like a toothbrush, body wash, shampoo, and conditioner. Bring your travel toothbrush, comb, brush, and any other necessary personal care supplies.
- ❖ **Bug repellent:** Use an efficient insect repellent to shield yourself from mosquitoes and other insects. Look for items with DEET or other suggested chemicals.
- ❖ **Vacation Documents Manager:** Keep all of your trip-related paperwork, tickets, and information in one convenient location by using a travel wallet or organizer.
- ❖ **Useful Shopping Bags:** For hauling groceries, beach necessities, or

souvenirs, a folding, reusable shopping bag can be useful.

Keep in mind to pack lightly and to leave room in your luggage for souvenirs or purchases you may make while traveling. To make sure you're ready for any unforeseen changes, check the weather prediction before you go. With a well-thought-out packing list and all the necessary travel items, you can concentrate on creating priceless experiences in the Mexican Caribbean.

Copyrighted material

Maps of Mexican Caribbean

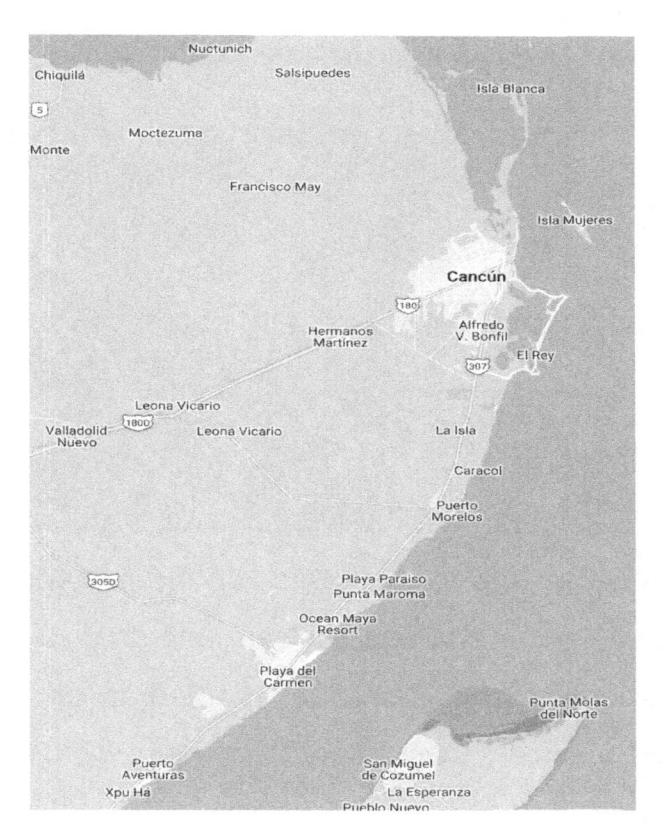

The Mexican Caribbean comprises several cities, including popular tourist destinations like Cancún, Playa del Carmen, Tulum, Cozumel, and Isla Mujeres, among others.

Conclusion and final Thought for an Unforgettable Experience

Take a minute to think back on the remarkable events and memories you've made as your time in the Mexican Caribbean comes to an end. The Mexican Caribbean is a realm of magic, offering an unmatched travel experience with its turquoise waters, immaculate beaches, and rich history.

You've enjoyed the taste of Mexican food during your journey while discovering the beauties of the Mayan ruins, cenotes, and environmental parks. The wonderful friendliness of the natives allowed you to fully experience their lively culture and traditions. Each experience, whether you were snorkeling in the Caribbean Sea, seeing colonial villages, or enjoying street food, has left an imprint on your heart.

All travelers are enthralled by the Mexican Caribbean, a region known for both its natural beauty and the kindness and warmth of its residents. You've had the delight of mingling with locals, exchanging smiles, and forging enduring connections that have cross-cultural and linguistic boundaries.

While you bring mementos and pictures home with you, keep in mind that the real value is in the relationships and experiences you've built. You have been given moments of wonder, peace, and adventure by the Mexican

Caribbean, and you will continue to find delight and inspiration from those memories in the days to come.

Maybe you've gained a fresh appreciation for history and archaeology or a passion for diving. Perhaps the flavors of Mexican food have made you yearn for more delectable dishes. Whatever the case, the Mexican Caribbean has made you appreciate the world's splendor and the depth of its many cultural traditions.

The Mexican Caribbean has served as both a destination and a starting point for adventure and self-discovery. It's a location where you learn to welcome new experiences, push past your comfort zone, and relish each of life's adventures.

Keep the Mexican Caribbean's spirit of exploration, friendliness, and beauty with you as you say goodbye. Let this magical land's memories serve as a prompt to treasure the world's wonders and look for fresh experiences wherever you go.

Although your journey is over, the Mexican Caribbean will always have a particular place in your heart. Let the wisdom, delight, and warmth of this place serve as a guide for your future journeys and daily life up until the day you return.

May the Mexican Caribbean's magic remain with you always, as a cherished chapter in your life's travel story. Farewell, and may your adventures continue to unfold with wonder and delight.

Enjoy your trip to the Mexican Caribbean and be safe!

Printed in Great Britain
by Amazon